ß

A FAREWELL
TO
GABO AND MERCEDES

A FAREWELL TO GABO AND MERCEDES

A Son's Memoir of Gabriel García Márquez and Mercedes Barcha

RODRIGO GARCIA

HarperVia

An Imprint of HarperCollinsPublishers

Grateful acknowledgment is made to the following for permission to reprint from previously published material:

Gabriel García Márquez, *One Hundred Years of Solitude*. Translated by Gregory Rabassa. English translation copyright © 1970 by Harper & Row Publishers, Inc. Reprinted by permission of HarperCollins Publishers.

Gabriel García Márquez, *The Autumn of the Patriarch*. Translated by Gregory Rabassa. English translation copyright © 1976 Harper & Row Publishers, Inc. Reprinted by permission of HarperCollins Publishers.

Gabriel García Márquez, *Love in the Time of Cholera*. Translated by Edith Grossman. English translation copyright © 1988 by Vintage Books, a division of Random House, Inc. Reprinted by permission of Penguin Random House.

Gabriel García Márquez, *The General in His Labyrinth*. Translated by Edith Grossman. English translation copyright © 1990 by Alfred A. Knopf, a division of Random House, Inc. Reprinted by permission of Penguin Random House.

Photography: Page 127 © Steven Pyke; page 147 © Pia Elizondo; all other photographs are reproduced by courtesy of the García Márquez Family Archive.

HarperCollins books may be purchased for educational, business, or sales promotional use. For information, please email the Special Markets Department at SPsales@harpercollins.com.

FIRST HARPERVIA EDITION PUBLISHED IN 2021

Designed by SBI Book Arts, LLC

Library of Congress Cataloging-in-Publication Data

Names: García, Rodrigo, 1959– author.
Title: A farewell to Gabo and Mercedes : a son's memoir / Rodrigo Garcia.
Description: First edition. | New York, NY : HarperVia, 2021.
Identifiers: LCCN 2021010396 | ISBN 9780063158337 (hardcover) | ISBN 9780063158313 (paperback) | ISBN 9780063158320 (ebook)
Subjects: LCSH: García Márquez, Gabriel, 1927–2014—Family. | Barcha, Mercedes. | García, Rodrigo, 1959– | Novelists, Colombian—Biography.
Classification: LCC PQ8180.17.A73 Z664817 2021 | DDC 863/.64—dc23
LC record available at https://lccn.loc.gov/2021010396

---

21 22 23 24 25   LSC   10 9 8 7 6 5 4 3 2 1

For my brother

CONTENTS

A FAREWELL
TO
GABO AND MERCEDES

PART ONE

Entonces fue al castaño, pensando en el circo, y mientras orinaba trató de seguir pensando en el circo, pero ya no encontró el recuerdo. Metió la cabeza entre los hombros, como un pollito, y se quedó inmóvil con la frente apoyada en el tronco del castaño. La familia no se enteró hasta el día siguiente, a las once de la mañana, cuando Santa Sofía de la Piedad fue a tirar la basura en el traspatio y le llamó la atención que estuvieran bajando los gallinazos.

—**Cien años de soledad**

Then he went to the chestnut tree, thinking about the circus, and while he urinated he tried to keep on thinking about the circus, but he could no longer find the memory. He pulled his head in between his shoulders like a baby chick and remained motionless with his forehead against the trunk of the chestnut tree. The family did not find him until the following day at eleven o'clock in the morning when Santa Sofía de la Piedad went to throw out the garbage in back and her attention was attracted by the descending vultures.

—*One Hundred Years of Solitude*

I

When my brother and I were children, my father made us promise to spend New Year's Eve of the year 2000 with him. He reminded us of that commitment several times throughout our adolescence, and his insistence was embarrassing to me. I eventually came to interpret it as his wish to still be alive on that date. He would be seventy-two, I would be forty, the twentieth century would come to an end. Those milestones could not seem further away when I was a teen. After my brother and I became adults, the promise was seldom mentioned, but we were indeed all together the night of the new millennium in my father's favorite city, Cartagena de Indias. "We had a deal, you and I," my father said to me shyly, perhaps then also somewhat embarrassed by his insistence. "That's right," I said, and we never spoke of it again. He lived another fifteen years.

When he was in his late sixties, I asked him what he thought about at night, after he turned out the lights. "I think that things are almost over." Then he added with a smile, "But there's still time. No need to get too worried just yet." His optimism was genuine, not just an attempt to comfort me. "You wake up one day and you're old. Just like that, with no warning. It's stunning," he added. "I heard years ago that there comes a time in the life of a writer when you are no longer able to write a long work of fiction. The head can no longer hold the vast architecture or navigate the perilous crossing of a lengthy novel. It's true. I can feel it now. So it will be shorter pieces from now on."

When he was eighty, I asked him what that was like.

"The view from eighty is astonishing, really. And the end is near."

"Are you afraid?"

"It makes me immensely sad."

When I think back on these moments, I am genuinely moved by how forthcoming he was, especially given the cruelty of the questions.

2

I call my mother on a weekday morning in March 2014, and she tells me that my father has been in bed with a cold for two days. This is not unusual for him, but she assures me that this time it's different. "He's not eating, and he won't get up. He's not himself. He's listless. Álvaro started like this," she adds, referring to a friend of my father's generation who died the previous year. "We're not getting out of this one" is her prognosis. After the call I am not alarmed, since my mother's forecast can be attributed to anxiety. She is well into a period of her life when old friends are dying with some frequency. And she's been hard hit by the recent loss of siblings, two of her youngest and dearest. Still, the call makes my imagination take flight. Is this how the end begins?

My mother, twice a cancer survivor, is due in Los Angeles for medical tests, so it is decided that my brother will fly in from Paris, where he lives, to Mexico City to be with our father. I will be with our mother in California. As soon as my brother arrives, my father's cardiologist and principal doctor tells him that my father has pneumonia and that the team would feel much more at ease if they could hospitalize him for further tests. It appears he had been suggesting that to my mother for at least a few days but that she had been reluctant. Perhaps she was scared of what a proper physical exam would uncover.

3

Phone conversations with my brother over the next few days allow me to form a picture of the hospital stay. When my brother checks my father in, the administrator jumps in her seat with excitement when she hears his name. "Oh, my God, the writer? Would you mind if I call my sister-in-law and tell her? She has to hear about this." He entreats her not to, and she yields, reluctantly. My father is placed in a relatively isolated room at one end of a hallway to protect his privacy, but within half a day doctors, nurses, orderlies, technicians, other patients, maintenance and cleaning personnel, and perhaps the administrator's sister-in-law make their way past his door to catch a glimpse of him. The hospital responds by limiting access to the area. Journalists have also begun to gather outside the main gate of the hospital, and the news is published that he is in grave condition. It's undeniable that we're being spoken to loud and clear: my father's illness will be partly a public affair. We cannot shut the door completely because much of the curiosity about him is from concern, admiration, and affection. When my brother and I were kids, our parents invariably referred to us, accurately or not, as the most well-behaved children in the world, so that expectation must be fulfilled. We must respond to this challenge, whether we have the strength for it or not, with civility and gratitude. We will need to do that while keeping my mother satisfied that the line between the public and the private, wherever we determine it to be given the circumstances, is strictly enforced. This has always been of enormous importance to her despite, or maybe because of, her addiction to the most salacious gossip shows on television. "We are not public figures," she likes to remind us. I know that I will not publish this memoir until she is unable to read it.

My brother has not seen my father for two months and finds him more disoriented than usual. My father doesn't recognize him and is anxious that he doesn't know where he is. He is put somewhat at ease by his driver and secretary, who take turns visiting with him, and one of them or the cook or the housekeeper spends the night with him at the hospital. There's no point in my brother staying because my father needs a more familiar face if he wakes up in the middle of the night. The doctors ask my brother how my father seems compared to a few weeks ago, since they cannot tell whether his state of mind is a product of his dementia or of his present weakness. He is making little sense and is unable to answer simple questions coherently. My brother confirms that although he seems somewhat worse, this is mostly how he has been for many months now.

This is one of the principal teaching hospitals in the country, so promptly the first morning a doctor comes around, shepherding a dozen interns. They cluster around the foot of the bed and listen as the doctor reviews the patient's condition and treatment, and it's clear to my brother that the young physicians had no idea whose room they had entered. Their growing realization can be seen from face to face as they observe him with weakly concealed curiosity. When the doctor asks if there are any questions, they all shake their heads no and follow him out like ducklings.

At least twice a day, as my brother leaves or arrives at the hospital, the crowd of reporters calls out to him. He is as unfailingly polite as a gentleman of the early nineteenth century and therefore constitutionally incapable of ignoring a human being who addresses him directly. So when asked, "Gonzalo, how is your father doing today?" he feels compelled to approach the group and becomes ensnared in an impromptu press conference. I see clips of it on television, and he is very capably, if tensely, working his way through it, fueled by sheer discipline. I encourage him to end this practice. I explain that when you see a photograph of a movie star walking sullenly out of a coffee shop, head bowed and ignoring the world around her, she is not being rude or arrogant. She is merely attempting to reach her car as quickly as possible with some dignity. He listens to me with the trepidation of someone being convinced to participate in a crime. When he finally adopts my recommendation, it is not without guilt, but after a little practice he admits that he could, in time, warm up to some of the heathen customs of show business.

Our father's pneumonia is responding to treatment, but scans reveal liquid accumulating in the pleural region as well as suspicious-looking areas in his lung and liver. These are not inconsistent with malignant tumors, but the doctors are reluctant to speculate without biopsies. The areas in question are difficult to access, so tissue would have to be collected under general anesthetic. Given his present state, there's the possibility that afterward he would be unable to breathe on his own and would be put on a respirator. It's the stuff of medical television shows, elementary but no less overwhelming. In Los Angeles, I present the situation to my mom, and as expected, she says no to a respirator. So no surgery and no biopsies and, without a cancer diagnosis, no treatment.

My brother and I discuss it and decide he should attempt to lean on one of the doctors, the resident or the lung surgeon perhaps, and force them to offer a prediction. My brother asks: "If either the lung or liver present malignant tumors"—if, always if—"what would be the prognosis?" He would have a few months, maybe longer, but only with chemotherapy. I describe the situation and symptoms to my father's oncologist and friend in Los

Angeles, and he says very calmly, "It's possibly lung cancer." Then he adds, "If that's what they suspect, take him
home and make him comfortable and, whatever you do,
never take him back to the hospital. The hospital stay
will beat up all of you." I consult with my father-in-law
in Mexico, also a physician, and his reaction is generally
the same: stay away from the hospital, make it easier for
my father and for us all.

4

I have to talk to my mother and confirm her worst fears that her husband of over half a century is terminally ill. I wait until we are alone on a Saturday morning. I start to explain the situation by summing up deliberately what we've been through and where we are now, and she listens and looks at me with what seems like mild disinterest, drowsily, as if she's hearing a story she's heard many times before. But when I get to the bottom line, I try to be brief and precise: it's very likely lung or liver cancer, or both, and he has only a few months to live. Before her expression betrays anything, her phone rings and she picks it up, which takes me completely by surprise. I observe her, stupefied, while she talks to someone in Spain, and I marvel at this living, breathing, textbook example of avoidance. It is, in its own way, beautiful as well as endearing. For all her strength and resources, she is just like everyone else. She keeps the call brief and hangs up and turns to me calmly and says, "And so?" as if we're discussing whether it's better to take an avenue or a side street. "Gonzalo will take him home the day after tomorrow. We should fly back to Mexico." She nods, taking it all in, then asks: "So this is it? For your father?"

"Yes, it seems that way."

"*Madre mía*," she says and lights up her electronic cigarette.

5

Writing about the death of loved ones must be about as old as writing itself, and yet the inclination to do it instantly ties me up in knots. I am appalled that I am thinking of taking notes, ashamed as I take notes, disappointed in myself as I revise notes. What makes matters emotionally turbulent is the fact that my father is a famous person. Beneath the need to write may lurk the temptation to advance one's own fame in the age of vulgarity. Perhaps it might be better to resist the call and to stay humble. Humility is, after all, my favorite form of vanity. But as with most writing, the subject matter choses you, and so resistance could be futile.

A few months earlier a friend asked how my dad was doing with his loss of memory. I told her he lives strictly in the present, unburdened by the past, free of expectations for the future. Forecasting based on previous experience, which is believed to be of evolutionary significance as well as one of the origins of storytelling, no longer plays a part in his life.

"So he doesn't know he's mortal," she concluded. "Lucky him."

Of course, the picture I painted for her is simplified. It is dramatized. The past still plays a part in his conscious life. He relies on the distant echo of his considerable interpersonal skills to ask anyone he meets a series of safe questions: "How is everything?" "Where are you living these days?" "How are your people?" Occasionally he'll venture an attempt at a more ambitious exchange and become disoriented in the middle of it, losing the thread of the idea or running out of words. The puzzled expression on his face, as well as the embarrassment that crosses it momentarily, like a puff of smoke in a breeze, betrays a past when conversation was as natural to him as breathing. Creative, funny, evocative, provocative conversation. Being a great *conversador* was almost as highly regarded among his oldest group of friends as being a good writer.

The future is also not completely behind him. Often at dusk he asks, "Where are we going tonight? Let's go out to a fun place. Let's go dancing. Why? Why not?" If you change the subject enough times, he moves on.

He recognizes my mother and addresses her as Meche, Mercedes, *La Madre*, or *La Madre Santa*. There were a few very difficult months not long ago when he remembered his lifelong wife but considered the woman in front of him, claiming to be her, to be an impostor.

"Why is she here giving orders and running the house if she is nothing to me?"

My mother reacted to this with anger.

"What is wrong with him?" she asked in disbelief.

"It's not him, Mom. It's dementia." She looked at me like I was trying to pull a fast one. Surprisingly, that period passed, and she regained her proper place in his mind as his principal companion. She is the last tether. His secretary, his driver, his cook, who have all worked in the house for years, he recognizes as familiar and friendly people who make him feel safe, but he no longer knows their names. When my brother and I visit, he looks at us long and hard, with uninhibited curiosity. Our faces ring a distant bell, but he cannot make us out.

"Who are those people in the next room?" he asks a housekeeper.

"Your sons."

"Really? Those men? *Carajo*. That's incredible."

There was an uglier period a couple of years earlier. My father was fully aware of his mind slipping away. He asked for help insistently, repeating time and time again that he was losing his memory. The toll of seeing a person in that state of anxiety and having to tolerate their endless repetitions over and over and over again is enormous. He would say, "I work with my memory. Memory is my tool and my raw material. I cannot work without it. Help me," and then he would repeat it in one form or another multiple times an hour for half an afternoon. It was grueling. That eventually passed. He regained some tranquility and would sometimes say, "I'm losing my memory, but fortunately I forget that I'm losing it," or "Everyone treats me like I'm a child. It's good that I like it."

His secretary tells me that one afternoon she found him standing alone in the middle of the garden, looking off into the distance, lost in thought.

"What are you doing out here, Don Gabriel?"

"Crying."

"Crying? You're not crying."

"Yes, I am. But without tears. Don't you realize that my head is now shit?"

On another occasion, he said to her: "This isn't my home. I want to go home. Home to my dad. I have a bed next to my dad's."

We suspect he was referring not to his father but to his grandfather, the colonel (and the inspiration for Colonel Aureliano Buendía), with whom he lived until he was eight. The colonel was the most influential man in his life. My father slept on a small mattress on the floor next to his bed. They never saw each other after 1935.

"That's the thing about your father," his secretary says to me. "Even ugly things he can talk about beautifully."

6

A woman who works for a medical equipment rental company delivers a hospital bed one morning and installs it in the guest bedroom under the supervision of my dad's secretary. Later, on the evening news, the woman sees an ambulance at the house returning my father from the hospital and realizes who the bed is for. The next day she writes a letter to us on behalf of her boss stating that it's an honor to provide the hospital bed for my father's use and that, of course, it will be free of charge. My mother's initial reaction is to decline, as she believes in always paying her own way. But we convince her to let it go. One less thing to deal with.

After my dad leaves the hospital, his discharge form is published in a tabloid. It appears that my brother may have dropped the document and that it was found by a visitor to the hospital, who in turn gave it as a gift to her daughter who is recuperating from surgery and who is an avid reader of my father's books. How it made it to print remains a mystery.

7

Ever since word got out that my father was hospitalized, press and supporters have started to gather outside the house. On the day he arrives from the hospital, close to one hundred people are there, and the city government has stationed police to maintain a perimeter around the front door. The ambulance carrying him backs into the garage, but it is too long to allow the garage door to close again. My brother, a housekeeper, and my father's secretary hold up bedsheets to protect him from being photographed as he is carried out the back of the ambulance and into the house. The published photo of my brother holding up sheets to protect whatever privacy remains infuriates me. Still, I remind myself, most of the people who are at the door are his readers and some serious press outlets, not tabloids.

Friends and doctors who come or leave are shamelessly accosted by journalists asking for updates. Family members usually drive into another garage and close the doors behind us, so we are spared. My dad's secretary tells me that on one of the very few occasions that week that my mother left the house, upon her return the garage door failed to open. She had no alternative but to walk about ten steps to the front door. As she stepped out of the car, the street fell dead silent in a spontaneous and remarkable show of respect. She walked the distance, head slightly bowed as if lost in thought, but apparently no more perturbed than if she were walking from her bedroom to the bathroom, unaware or unconcerned that the climate changed for her. My father said many times that she was the most surprising person he ever met.

We decide that my father cannot be placed in the master bedroom, where his care will disrupt my mother's sleep. He is placed down the hall from her, in a guest room that also serves as a screening room. Decades ago, it was a large terrace where high school students gathered to smoke, but it was eventually enclosed.

After he is installed in the hospital bed, my father's first words, delivered through a raspy whisper and hard to make out, are "I want to go home." My mother explains that he is home. He looks around with something like disappointment, apparently recognizing nothing. He takes his right hand up shakily to his face in a gesture that is very much his. The hand lands on the forehead and then slides down very slowly over the eyes, closing them shut. A frown and tightly pursed lips round it out. It's a gesture that he uses as a sign of exhaustion or concentration or when he is overwhelmed by something he just heard, usually something to do with a person's hardship. We see it frequently over the next few days.

My father will be taken care of by his two regular aides and two nurses who work in two shifts. The day nurse is impressive. She was recommended by the hospital when my father was released. She is in her late thirties, married, no children, cordial, even-tempered, confident, and she radiates common sense. Her logs are detailed and neatly written in longhand, medications and supplies impeccably laid out, curtains in the room pulled and drawn throughout the day to maintain only a soothing amount of brightness in the room. The beauty of witnessing someone who is outstanding at what she does, in conjunction with the comfort brought about by the support of an empathetic health worker, makes her a compelling presence. She is also affectionate with her patient, often addressing him as *mi amor* or *chiquito hermoso* (lovely little one). Only once do I see her flustered. In revising a doctor's latest instructions, she finds either what she considers an incomplete form or an inconsistency in the papers regarding my father's "Do Not Resuscitate" orders. For a good half hour everything is put aside as she reviews the documents while leaving phone messages. Finally, she speaks with the cardiologist and is satisfied with what she is told. After a final set of initials from my mother and my assurances that everything reflects everyone's wishes, she returns to her routine, visibly relieved.

Every now and then my father awakes, and it's cause

for excitement around him. Family, caretakers, and not infrequently a visiting doctor are happy to interact with him. We ask him questions, listen carefully to his answers, and encourage conversation. We are delighted that he's alert, and for the doctors and nurses there is the thrill of chatting with the legendary maestro. He speaks with a deliberateness that makes you forget, in the happiness of the good moment, that he is years deep into dementia and that the man we are talking to is hardly there at all, can hardly make sense of any of it, is hardly himself.

A few times a day his weight is shifted in the bed, and he is massaged and stretched. If he is awake, I can see a sleepy kind of pleasure come over him. One afternoon, a young doctor—who was the chief intern at the hospital, son of a Colombian father—stops by. He asks my father how he feels, and the answer is *"Jodido"* (Screwed). The nurse informs, as part of the long rundown, that my father has skin chafing and that they have been *"cuidando sus genitales"* (taking care of his genitals), applying cream to the area. My father is listening and makes a face of appalled horror. But he's smiling, and his expression doesn't lie: he's joking. Then, just to be clear, he adds: *"Quiere decir, mis huevos"* (You mean, my balls). The room is in stitches. His humor has survived dementia, it seems. It's part and parcel of the most essential him. Overall, my father was a modest man with respect to his physique. Timid, even. But I don't think he would have found any lack of dignity in how he was taken care of. He would have been very touched by the affection he received.

When it's time for the nurses' change of shift, the two nurses and two aides, as well as one or both housekeepers, gather in the room for a few minutes. My father's secretary comments, looking at his feet during a change of bedsheets, that she had heard he has beautiful feet but she had never seen them. The women all look at them and agree. Where on earth she could have heard that, I have no idea. I'd rather not ask.

The sound of a chorus of female voices sometimes stirs him awake. He opens his eyes, and they light up as soon as the women turn to him and address him with affection and praise. On one of those occasions, I am in the next room when I hear the group of women laughing loudly. I walk in to ask what's happening. I'm told my father opened his eyes, took a patient look at the women, and said calmly: "*No me las puedo tirar a todas*" (I can't fuck all of you).

A moment later, when my mother walks in, her voice and her presence entrance him.

8

Throughout my childhood, both my parents took naps in the afternoon, almost without exception. Every now and then my father would ask us to wake him up if he slept past a certain time. My brother and I learned at a very early age that it was a risky assignment. If you were standing too close when you told him to wake up or if, God forbid, you nudged him, he would be startled to the point of waking up screaming, waving his arms around trying to protect himself from something or someone, terrified, gasping for air. It would take several moments for him to relocate himself in this world. So we developed a system: stand at the door of the bedroom and call out his name in a calm, quiet monotone. He would still jolt awake sometimes, but more often than not he wouldn't. And if the reaction was that of horror, we were able to retreat to the hallway quickly.

After a good awakening, he would rub his face with both his hands as if slowly washing it, then call with his favorite nickname for us, *Perro Burro* (Donkey Dog).

He'd wave us over, order us to kiss him, and then proceed
to ask: "What is new? How is life?" It was not unusual
also to hear him at night moaning and gasping and my
mother shaking his shoulder vigorously to wake him up. I
once asked him after a turbulent nap what he was dream-
ing. He closed his eyes to retrieve it.

"It's a beautiful day and I am in a canoe without oars,
drifting very slowly, peacefully, down a placid river."

Where is the nightmare in that, I asked.

"I have no idea."

I know he must, however. Despite his persistent denial
of anything deliberately symbolic in his writing, and his
disdain for any academic or highbrow theories that could
shed light on imagery in his stories, he knows that he is a
slave to the unconscious, like everyone. He knows things
are standing in for other things. And like so many writers, he is obsessed with loss and with its greatest manifes-
tation, death. Death as order and disorder, as logic and
nonsense, as the inevitable and the unacceptable.

9

In his early seventies, during and after several rounds of chemotherapy, my father wrote his memoirs. The project was initially conceived as a series of books, the first one starting with his earliest memories and ending with his move to Paris at age twenty-seven to work as a correspondent. But after the initial one, he wrote no others, mainly because he became fearful that writing about periods of success could evolve, like so many of the memoirs of the famous, into little more than name-dropping. A night with so-and-so, visiting a famous painter's studio, plotting with this or that head of state, breakfast with a charismatic insurgent.

"Only the first book would be of any interest, to me, anyway," he said, "because it covers the years that made me a writer."

In another context he once said, "Nothing interesting happened to me after the age of eight."

That's how old he was when he moved away from his grandparents' house, the town of Aracataca, and the world that inspired his early writing. His first few books, he admitted, were trial runs for *One Hundred Years of Solitude.*

In researching his memoirs, he reached out to friends from as far back as preschool, many of whom he had not seen or heard from since. In some cases, he was only able to speak to a son or daughter or wife because the friend had already passed away. He had expected that some would have died along the way, but he was taken aback by those who had died in recent years: men who had lived entire, relatively happy and productive lives and had died in their seventies, the average life expectancy in the world. The deaths of these men his own age were not tragic, simply the end of natural life cycles. After this period, he took to saying, "A lot of people are dying that weren't dying before," and he enjoyed the laughter it provoked.

10

Despite his gregarious nature and an apparent comfort with public life, my father was quite a private, sometimes even secretive, person. This is not to say that he was unable to enjoy fame or that, after decades of adulation, he was unscathed by narcissism, but still there was always in him a suspicion of celebrity and of literary success. He reminded us (and himself) several times over the years that neither Tolstoy, Proust, or Borges ever won the Nobel Prize, nor did three of his favorite writers: Virginia Woolf, Juan Rulfo, and Graham Greene. Often it seemed to him that his success was not something he had achieved but something that had happened to him. Up until late in life, as his memory was fading, he never reread his books for fear that he would find them embarrassingly wanting and that it would paralyze him creatively.

11

I fly back to Los Angeles for a couple of days to continue work on a film I am editing. It's a story of fathers
and sons, and the long climactic scene, which we are
working on, involves the death of the father through a
series of circumstances for which the son may be partly
to blame. There is a confrontation followed by something
like an accident, a dying scene, a carrying and washing of
the corpse, and a final ritual of sorts that obliterates the
body, erasing the father forever from the surface of the
earth. The fact that I have to work on this as my father
is in his final weeks is a grim coincidence that is not lost
on anyone. I embrace it like it's just something that has
to be weathered and accepted: God's sense of humor. But
as time goes by, I can't pretend that working on these
scenes isn't grating. It's debilitating. I hate myself for having written such a story. I overeat, chocolate mostly, to
deaden some of the pain. Maybe the only story worth
telling is one that makes you laugh. I'll do that next time,
I'm sure. Or perhaps not.

For a few years after I started directing films, I was often asked what artists had influenced me. I dutifully fired off a list of names, partly original, mostly obvious, until the day came when I realized I was being dishonest. No director, writer, poet—no painting or song—has exerted much influence on me compared to my parents, my brother, my wife, my daughters. Most things worth knowing are still learned at home.

12

When I return to Mexico, my father has been back home just over a week, but already my mother seems very tired. She asks me if I really think it'll be months, and she asks in a way that makes it clear she doesn't feel like she can stomach that time frame. My father's convalescence in the house is nevertheless a quiet one. He's in a room away from the main bedrooms, tended to day and night, and he appears generally at peace. In the rest of the house, it would seem nothing out of the ordinary is happening. For my mother, however, the clock is ticking ruthlessly slow in that room, and as loudly as cathedral bells.

I say to her that I don't think it'll be that long, but my estimate is based on nothing but my desire to comfort her. The next morning his cardiologist returns, and after a long examination of my father he changes his estimate. It will not be months now, most likely weeks. Three, maybe, at the most. My mom listens in silence, smoking, perhaps equal parts relieved and dismayed.

Later, a gerontologist of about forty stops by to advise on end-stage care. He is the youngest of the many doctors that we've dealt with recently, which is unexpected if we presume that the young should be unable to understand the trials of old age. My mother interrogates him like she does everyone. He reveals that he has suffered from a lymphoma that is in remission, and I see him in a whole new light. He looks vulnerable suddenly, and self-conscious. The possibility that he may be in more imminent danger than his patients several decades older must be disquieting. He says that when the time comes, if we want to move things along, my father's water drip could be interrupted. A handful of countries, he informs us, consider water a human right that can never be denied a patient under any circumstances. Mexican law differs, and it is not uncommon for family members to interrupt hydration when the end is very near. The patient by then is usually sedated, he says, and will not suffer. We listen in silence, like we're watching a strange monologue in an experimental play. The ideas are intriguing and absurd. Practical, compassionate, murderous.

13

My mother and I are sitting together watching cable news when she says to me out of the blue: "We have to be prepared because it's going to be a zoo." She's referring to the reaction in the media and among readers and friends the world over when my father dies. Many started to call or write as soon as the news broke of his hospitalization. Then a few outlets stated that he had come home to spend his last days. He's eighty-seven years old, so it's not greatly speculative to suppose that he may in fact be in trouble.

We decide, together with my brother, that as soon as my father dies, we will make a handful of calls to journalists we know personally. It's a short list: two newspapers in Colombia; one is the most influential in that country; the other is the one where my father began his career in his early twenties. In Mexico, we settle on one of the foremost journalists in the country, a woman who has news shows on both television and radio. We will also call a few close friends who can spread the news as they see fit. His agent and friend is one of them, of course, as are a couple in Barcelona, as well as one of his brothers, the point person for the family in Colombia. They have already been warned that we're close to the end.

PART TWO

Entonces cruzó los brazos contra el pecho y empezó a oír las voces radiantes de los esclavos cantando la salve de las seis en los trapiches, y vio por la ventana el diamante de Venus en el cielo que se iba para siempre, las nieves eternas, la enredadera nueva cuyas campánulas amarillas no vería florecer el sábado siguiente en la casa cerrada por el duelo, los últimos fulgores de la vida que nunca más, por los siglos de los siglos, volvería a repetirse.

—**El general en su laberinto**

Then he crossed his arms over his chest and began to listen to the radiant voices of the slaves singing the six o'clock Salve in the mills, and through the window he saw the diamond of Venus in the sky that was dying forever, the eternal snows, the new vine whose yellow bellflowers he would not see bloom on the following Saturday in the house closed in mourning, the final brilliance of life that would never, through all eternity, be repeated again.

—*The General in His Labyrinth*

14

I fly to Los Angeles again to spend a few more days in the cutting room. My second night at home, I go to bed early, but after I turn out the lights I'm worried that the phone will ring in the middle of the night and scare the wits out of me. It does both. I hear my brother's voice on the other end, sounding deliberately calm.

"Hey. He has a high fever. The doctor says you better come back."

After I hang up, I book an early flight on my phone and I lie awake in the dark. I am overcome by a great sadness for my brother, my mother, and me. When my brother and I were children growing up in Mexico and Spain, the rest of the family on both sides was in Colombia, so we had a strong sense of the four of us as a unit, a club of four. Now the club is about to lose its first member. It's almost crushing.

On the flight the next day, for a moment I am not sure if I'm flying to or from Mexico City, such has been the daze of the last few days. Once at the airport, while walking between immigration and baggage claim, I dial my brother.

"He has less than twenty-four hours," he says.

Fuck. How did we go from "He has only months" to "It's more likely a few weeks" to twenty-four hours? After dozens of conversations with nurses, surgeons, oncologists, lung specialists, chief residents, and gerontologists, all of whom sternly avoided speculation, the boldness of this new prediction is ruthless. My father's cardiologist has taken pains at every turn to explain the difference between the possible and the probable. Now we are in the definitive. The authority with which they can assert that his life will be over within a day appears to be remarkable, but apparently there's no major math to it. The kidneys are failing. Potassium is building up in the bloodstream. It will stop the heart. It's the same end of hundreds of millions of individuals before him. Life, as old as it is and as many times as it has been lived, continues to be mercifully unpredictable. Death, when it orbits this closely, seldom disappoints.

I walk toward the baggage carousel with tears running down my face.

15

I ask the day nurse to let me know if she sees in my father any change or symptom that may indicate to her that the end is near. I add that there is no pressure to provide a warning, but that if she sees anything, I will appreciate it. My brother's wife and their children have flown in from their home in Paris, and my wife and our daughters will be flying in the next morning.

That afternoon, while my mother naps, I work a little in my father's study. I look out toward the house, and it's remarkable how quiet it is. I walk out to the garden and stand very still and marvel that nothing betrays the fact that a person's life is ending in an upstairs bedroom.

The house is in a neighborhood developed in the forties and fifties by the architect Luis Barragán. It was originally comprised of modernist residences that were joined, in the seventies and eighties, by mansions of dubious architectural merit. My father was never enthusiastic about the area. But he found a house by an outlier, Manuel Parra, who created his own style—a fusion of Mexican colonial,

Spanish, and Moorish styles, often incorporating doors, window frames, and stonemasonry salvaged from demolitions. Despite the unlikely list of ingredients, the homes he designed feel genuine and are welcoming. My father always admired his work and thought it fun, if not a little perverse, to inhabit one of his homes in this neighborhood of brainy modernist and gaudy marble palaces.

In my teens, I would frequently lie on my back on the grass and look up at the sky and feel strongly attached to this garden. (Even then I was aware that it was about as unexciting a favorite spot as a boy could have.) From that vantage point, the end of the day was pleasurable. For those who have spent years in Mexico City, it is no surprise that often the late afternoons can be unique. Sometimes, after the rain, there is a new transparency and a lovely fragrance in the air, and the Ajusco peak can be seen in the distance, and there comes over the city a sudden stillness, and the feeling of not being in the polluted, chaotic megalopolis, but in the splendid valley that it once was, and for a moment there is a sense of both longing and possibility. My brother and my sister-in-law were married here in sunny weather, and during the reception an hour later a furious storm pummeled the tents with hail the size of marbles. My father was delighted. As he saw it, it could only be a harbinger of good things. They've been married over thirty years.

A party was also held in this garden for my father's

sixtieth birthday, and he chose to invite only friends of his generation. Some younger friends were offended, and they confronted him with it. He was firm with them, unapologetic: the house could not accommodate everyone in his very large life, so he chose only people in his age group. In private he was mortified that he had hurt anyone's feelings.

I walk around the ground floor of the house. The kitchen has been cleaned up after lunch, and the living room looks like it has always looked. That is not precise, of course, but the furniture, the art, and the trinkets have accumulated in easy layers decade after decade, forming something both vaguely new and reassuringly old. Dating any of it with any accuracy is impossible. There is a small, ancient rock formation that resembles a flower with petals as sharp as paring knives that was already there in the early eighties; a handwritten poem by Rafael Alberti that must be from the seventies, after his return to Madrid from forty years in exile; a self-portrait by Álejandro Obregón with shrapnel holes in it (drunk one night, the artist shot his painted self in the eye with a revolver, angry that his adult children were fighting over ownership of the painting); and a book of photographs by Jacques-Henri Lartigue that I've been looking at since I was twelve.

For about twenty-five years, there was a parrot in the house that could sometimes be heard whistling to an absent pretty girl when a door shut or a phone rang in the afternoon; after its exertion, it would settle in to rest quietly for the rest of the day. Not many of us paid much attention to the bird, but everyone was heartbroken when it died.

16

I walk upstairs and look into my father's room. The day nurse takes notes while the aide reads a magazine. My father is perfectly still, in something like sleep, but the room feels different from the rest of the house. For all the tranquility, time now seems to move faster here, like it's in a rush, impatient to make time for more time. It's disconcerting.

Standing near the foot of the bed, I look at him, diminished as he is, and I feel like both his son (his little son) and his father. I am acutely aware that I have a unique overview of his eighty-seven years. The beginning, the middle, and the end are all there in front of me, unfolding like an accordion book.

It's a dizzying sensation to know the destiny of a human being. Of course, the years before I was born are a concoction of things told to me by him or his siblings or my mother, or recounted by relatives, friends, journalists, and biographers, and embellished by my own imagination: My father as a boy of six playing goalkeeper in a soccer game and feeling that he was playing very well, better than usual. A year or two later, looking at a solar eclipse without a proper glass and forever losing the sight at the center of his left eye. Watching from the door of his grandparents' house as men walked by carrying the dead body of a man, and the wife walking behind them holding a child in one hand and the husband's severed head in the other. Spitting into his fruit gelatin or eating plantain chips from his shoe to discourage his many brothers and sisters from poaching his food. In adolescence, a trip up the Magdalena River toward boarding school, feeling miserably alone. From his time in Paris, an afternoon he visited a woman and tried to extend the visit so as to be asked for dinner, since he was broke and hadn't eaten in days. After that failed, rummaging through her garbage on the way out and eating out of it. (He told this to others in front of me when I was fifteen, and I felt as embarrassed as an adolescent can feel by their parent.) There was also in Paris a melancholy Chilean girl, Violeta Parra, that he occasionally ran into at get-togethers of Latin American expatriates. She wrote and sang beautiful, heart-wrenching songs and eventually took her own life. One afternoon in Mexico City in 1966, he walked up to the room where my mother read in bed and announced to her that he had just written the death of Colonel Aureliano Buendía.

"I've killed the colonel," he said to her, distraught.

She knew what that meant to him, and they sat together in silence with the sad news.

Even in the long period of great and rare literary acclaim, wealth, and access, there were ugly days, of course. The death of Álvaro Cepeda at forty-six from cancer, and the assassination of journalist Guillermo Cano by drug cartels at sixty-one. The deaths of two brothers (the youngest of sixteen siblings), the alienating aspect of celebrity, the loss of memory and the inability to write that came with it. He eventually reread his books in his old age, and it was like reading them for the first time. "Where on earth did all this come from?" he once asked me. He continued to read them until the end, eventually recognizing them as familiar books by the cover but understanding very little of their content. Sometimes, when closing a book, he would be surprised to find his photograph on the back cover, so he would reopen it and attempt to read it again.

Standing there, at the foot of his bed, I'd like to think that his brain, despite the dementia (and perhaps aided by the morphine), is still the cauldron of creativity that it always was. Fractured, perhaps, unable to return to thoughts or to sustain story lines, but still active. His imagination was always prodigiously fertile. Six generations of the Buendía family make up *One Hundred Years of Solitude*, but he had enough material for two more generations. He decided not to include it for fear the novel would be too long and tiresome. He thought great discipline was one of the cornerstones of writing a novel, particularly when it came to framing the shape and limits of the tale. He disagreed with those who said it was a freer, and therefore easier, form than a screenplay or a short story. It was imperative, he argued, that the novelist draft his or her own rigorous road map in order to traverse what he referred to as "the treacherous terrain of a novel."

The journey from Aracataca in 1927 to this day in Mexico City in 2014 is about as long and extraordinary a journey as a person can have, and those dates on a tombstone could never begin to encompass it. From where I'm standing, it looks like one of the most fortunate and privileged lives ever lived by a Latin American. He'd be the first to agree.

17

On Wednesday night, sleep is choppy. I am anxious that I will be woken up by a knock on the door telling me that he has died. I get up at dawn and walk to his room, and the nurse informs me that he didn't stir during the night. He is in the exact position I last saw him, breathing almost imperceptibly. I wonder if the nurses are still stretching and repositioning him to avoid bedsores or whether we are beyond that. I shower and dress and return to the room. Now, in the morning light, he looks like someone else, an austere twin brother with gaunt features and translucent skin that I don't know as well. I feel differently about this guy. Detached. Maybe that is the purpose of the transformation, to help you uncouple, just as a simple look at your newborn instantly triggers feelings of attachment.

In the kitchen I sit alone at the table with the silent cook, who has worked on and off in the house for decades and whom my father enjoyed very much because of her fiery temper. She gives me a look at one point but says nothing. Soon she steps out to look in on her boss "in case he needs anything," she says.

After breakfast I can hear the *vallenatos* playing in my father's room. It's his favorite musical form, and he always returned to it after periods of infidelity with chamber music or pop ballads. Even as his memory loss accelerated, he could, if given the opening verse, recite from memory many of the poems of the Spanish Golden Age. After that ability waned, he could still sing along to his favorite songs. The *vallenato* is an art form so particular to the world he was born into that even in his last months, incapable of remembering practically anything, his eyes would light up with excitement at the opening accordion notes of a classic one. His secretary would often play long compilations of them as he sat in his study, happily trapped in a time tunnel. So now, in the last couple of days, the nurses have started to play them loudly in his room, windows wide open. They fill the house. Some of them are by his *compadre* Rafael Escalona. In this context, I find them haunting. They take me as far back in his life as anything possibly can, and I travel through it and back to the present, where they play like a final lullaby.

My dad greatly admired and envied songwriters for their ability to say so much and so eloquently with so few words. While writing *Love in the Time of Cholera*, he submitted himself to a steady diet of Latin pop songs of love lost or unrequited. He said to me that the novel would be nowhere as melodramatic as many of those songs, but that he could learn much from them about the techniques with which they evoked feelings. He was never a snob about art forms and enjoyed the work of people as diverse as Béla Bartók and Richard Clayderman. He once walked by as I was watching Elton John playing his best songs on television, alone at the piano. My dad was only vaguely aware of him, but the music stopped him in his tracks, and he eventually sat down and watched all of it, enthralled. "*Carajo*, this guy is an incredible *bolerista*," he said. A singer of *boleros*. It was very much like him to refer something back to his own culture. He was never intimidated by Eurocentric references that were common everywhere. He knew that great art could blossom in an apartment building in Kyoto or in a rural county in Mississippi, and he had the unwavering conviction that any remote and rickety corner of Latin America or the Caribbean could stand in powerfully for the human experience.

He was an omnivorous reader, and he enjoyed things like *¡Hola!* magazine, the case studies of a physician, the memoirs of Muhammad Ali, or a thriller by Frederick Forsyth, whose political views he deplored. Among his less heralded literary loves was Thornton Wilder, and *Ides of March* was on his nightstand for what seemed like half my lifetime. There were also dictionaries and language reference books, which he picked at constantly. I never once saw him not know the meaning of a word in Spanish, and he could also offer a reasonable guess at its etymology. I was once struggling to remember the word that describes the critical interpretation of a text, and for a moment he was beside himself, putting everything aside in a frantic effort to retrieve it from the tip of his tongue. His delight was palpable as he quickly called out, "Exegesis!" It was not an obscure word, but far removed from his world. It was a word that, in his view, belonged to academia and to intellectual concerns, which were all a little suspect to him.

18

Later that morning, a bird is found dead inside the house. The back porch had been enclosed a few years earlier to make a visiting and dining area overlooking the garden. The walls are glass, so it is surmised that the bird flew in, became disoriented, crashed against the glass, and fell dead on the sofa, precisely on the spot where my dad sat regularly. My father's secretary informs me that the employees in the house are divided into two groups: those who think it's a bad omen and want the bird thrown in a trash can, and those who think it's a good omen and want it buried among the flowers. The Trashists have taken the upper hand, and the bird is already in a garbage can outside the kitchen. After further debate, the bird is placed in a corner of the garden, above ground for now, while its final destination is decided. It is eventually buried near the parrot, in a plot that also includes a puppy. The existence of the pet cemetery was always kept from my father, who would have been perturbed by it.

19

We are gathered at noon, my mother, my brother, and his family, who flew in from France the previous evening. Also newly arrived from Bogotá in the hours before dawn is our cousin from our mother's side, who lived with us for long periods as a child and is as close to my parents as a daughter. The mood is surprisingly light, I suppose because no one is inclined to mourn the living and because it's a reunion, after all, and mostly of young people.

Through the glass doors I see my father's secretary come out of his office in the back of the garden and move quickly toward us. I catch her eye, and she calls out that the nurse wants to talk to me. She is trying not to alarm anyone, but it's clear that something has come up. I walk out as calmly as I can, but the room falls silent.

As I am approaching the guest room, the day nurse walks out to meet me. "His heart has stopped," she says nervously. As I walk into the room, I initially find my father looking no different than he did less than ten minutes ago, but after only a few seconds I realize how wrong I am. He looks devastated, as if something had hit him—a train, a truck, lightning—a thing that caused no injuries other than knocking the life clean out of him. I walk around the bed and up to him and curse under my breath. The nurse is alternately checking for a pulse with a stethoscope and dialing a doctor. I can tell that she is momentarily worried that my anger may be directed at her for not giving me a warning as I requested, but since I am not really engaging her directly, she moves on from that preoccupation.

She finally reaches my dad's cardiologist. She explains that there has been no heartbeat for almost three minutes. The doctor asks to speak to me. He gives me his condolences and offers to come to the house, but I know he is far away that day, on a day off, and I tell him it's not necessary. We had already agreed that when the time came, he would alert the chief resident at the hospital to come to the house to fill out the paperwork. I phone downstairs. My mother answers and I say, "His heart stopped," and I can hardly get through the third word without my voice breaking, but I think she hangs up before she can hear it. I return to my father. His head lies to the side, his mouth is slightly agape, and he looks as frail as a person can look. Seeing him like this, in this most human scale, is both terrifying and comforting.

I see my mom walking up the stairs and toward the

guest room, followed by my brother and his family. She is usually the slowest mover, but it's evident that everyone has chosen to let her lead. Over the past few weeks, she has relied on my brother and me for dozens of decisions, but when she walks into the room and sees my father, it strikes me how their decades together give her complete authority over this moment. They were strangers to each other once, which is unimaginable. They first met as neighbors, and when he was fourteen and she was ten, he playfully asked her to marry him, and she ran home crying. On the day of their wedding, fifty-seven years and twenty-eight days before this moment, but at the exact same time of day, she would not put on the dress until she knew he was outside the church so there would be no chance of being left at the altar in a wedding gown.

My mom's first instinct as she crosses through the door is to take charge. The nurse and the aide are propping my father's head up and working to keep his mouth shut by tying his jaw with a towel around the head. "Tighter," my mother calls out as she approaches the bed. "That's it." She looks my father up and down with detachment as if he were her patient. She pulls the sheet up to his chest, smooths it over, puts her hand on his. She looks at his face and caresses his forehead, and for a moment she is unfathomable. Then a brief convulsion overcomes her, and she erupts into tears. "*Pobrecito, ¿verdad?*" (Poor little thing, isn't he?) Even before her own pain and sadness comes a profound sympathy for him. I've seen her cry only three times before in my whole life. This one lasts no more than a few seconds, but it has the power of a burst of machine-gun fire.

The next few moments are a blur. My mother walks away and sits outside in the hallway. For the first time in months, she lights up a cigarette rather than an e-cigarette. I ask the nurse to put my father's dentures back on, before his jaw sets, and it's a relief how much better he looks with them in place. My brother and his family stand around the bed, distraught. His oldest son and daughter knew my father well when they were little, before his memory started to fade. They seem inconsolable. Word spreads, and in an order that I can no longer recall, one person after another who works in the house makes their way to the door or to his bedside and looks on in disbelief. There is no apparent self-consciousness or awkwardness in expressing pain or grief in front of the others. The surroundings fade away and each and every person has their own singular encounter, not just with the deceased but also with the event itself, as if death were a communal property. Nobody can be denied their relationship to it, their membership in that society. And death as something that is, rather than as the lack of something, is sobering to behold. That seems to be the case even for the nurses in the room. They go about their business, but it seems to me that they are now in their heads, unable to avoid reflection. It's not an occurrence that must ever get old.

20

The day nurse and the aide clean and prepare my father's body for the journey to the mortuary. The nurse asks my mom if there are clothes she would like my father to wear. She says no, so the nurse suggests a simple shroud. My mother produces a fine, white, embroidered bedsheet and hands it over with little ceremony.

While my father is being prepared, a physician fills in the necessary papers for the death certificate. We realize the calls to the press must wait. A close friend is in the air at that very moment, traveling from Colombia to say goodbye to my father, as is a friend from Mexico who is flying back from her family holiday. But I am mostly concerned about my teenage daughters, who are also in midflight with my wife, traveling from Los Angeles. I don't want them to land and turn on their phones and read that their grandfather is already dead. So we decide to stay put and call no one until everyone lands and checks in with us. It would make my dad laugh. "*Vestidos y alborotados*" (All dressed up and nowhere to go).

When I look into the room again, my father's entire body is wrapped from his feet to the base of the skull. The bed has been lowered so he lays flat, except for a very thin pillow that props up his head ever so slightly. His face has been scrubbed, and the towel tied around his head has been removed. The jaw is set, and the dentures are in place. He looks pale and serious but at peace. His thin gray curls flat against his head remind me of a patrician bust. My niece places yellow roses on his abdomen. They were his favorite flowers, and he believed they brought him good luck.

Over the next few hours we sit with my mother who, as she often does, turns on the news to distract herself. On TV is a show about the life of Octavio Paz, the poet and diplomat who died a few years earlier and was a casual friend of my parents. My mom watches a few minutes of the show, but it's clear from her expression that her thoughts are with the documentaries she suspects she will be watching in the coming days and weeks.

Suddenly she says, to no one in particular, that my dad is probably already with Álvaro, the friend who died the previous year, "*tomando whisky y hablando paja*" (drinking whiskey and talking trash).

The house phone rings, and she answers it herself, which she seldom does. It's a friend they do not see very often. He's calling to inquire about my dad's health, and he's offering any help that may be needed. My mother listens patiently and thanks him perfunctorily, but at the first opportunity tells him that my father has already died. It's not necessary to hear him on the other side to imagine the shock of the news, especially the matter-of-fact tone in which it is delivered. She goes on to explain that it all happened just in the last hour, as if she were talking about a food delivery. My niece and nephews, who know her well, are appalled but also struggling to control their laughter. Once I give them a knowing look, they lose it and have to walk away.

21

The friend from Colombia has already landed, but I don't find out until the doorbell rings and I am told that he is downstairs. I descend and walk briskly into the kitchen and almost stumble into him, and without a proper greeting I blurt out that my father has died. He is one of my dad's oldest cronies, and I have blindsided him. He's stunned and speechless and his eyes glaze over, as if revisiting in his mind a lifetime of friendship in a matter of seconds. I think to myself that I must be very tired and tense to break the news so clumsily and that I have to do better.

The friend who is returning from her holiday also checks in, and finally my wife lands and calls me from the airplane. I tell her the news and her sadness touches me, so much so that I am incapable of talking to my daughters. I want to wait until I see them in person.

I call a few friends and relatives, and each call is harder than the previous one. It's a group that has been kept up to date, so nobody is surprised, but everyone is silent or almost silent over the line. It's more a vacuum than a silence. Most of them have the mission to call other people, and they set off to do so without much comment. My father's agent of almost fifty years only says, "*Qué barbaridad*," and she says it like things in the world that have forever been impossible have finally come to be. In my mind I can see her face, eyes closed, engrossed in the idea of it, attempting to go deep inside herself, where the unimaginable might gradually become real. "*Qué barbaridad*," she repeats. "That's terrible," then we hang up. With many of my father's lifelong friends I perceive a similar reaction. Beyond the sadness is the disbelief that such an exuberant, expansive man, forever intoxicated with life and with the travails of the living, has been extinguished.

I sit down to call the news outlets we had agreed on, but it being late in the day on a Good Thursday, reaching directors of news organizations in Catholic countries proves impossible. It's almost as slow a news cycle as Christmas Eve, and so everyone is away until Monday. We had been going stir-crazy, sitting around for almost two hours, prisoners of news everyone is expecting us to deliver, and now there's no one to hear it. Finally, we ask the friend who just flew in from her family holiday, who is a radio personality with a large following, to announce it on social media. It's only a matter of minutes before the home phones and cell phones start to ring, and the number of reporters, well-wishers, and police officers at the front door multiplies.

PART THREE

Amaneció muerta el jueves santo. La enterraron en una cajita que era apenas más grande que la canastilla en que fue llevado Aureliano, y muy poca gente asistió al entierro, en parte porque no eran muchos quienes se acordaban de ella, y en parte porque ese mediodía hubo tanto calor que los pájaros desorientados se estrellaban como perdigones contra las paredes y rompían las mallas metálicas de las ventanas para morirse en los dormitorios.

—**Cien años de soledad**

They found her dead on the morning of Good Thursday. They buried her in a coffin that was not much larger than the basket in which Aureliano had arrived, and very few people were at the funeral, partly because there were not many left who remembered her, and partly because it was so hot that noon that the birds in their confusion were flying into walls like day buckshot and breaking through screens to die in the bedrooms.

—One Hundred Years of Solitude

22

Shortly after the news of my father's death is made public, his secretary receives an email from a friend she hasn't talked to in a long time. The friend wanted to know if we were aware that Úrsula Iguarán, one of his most famous characters, also died on a Good Thursday. She has included the passage from his novel in her email, and in rereading it, my dad's secretary discovers that after Úrsula's death, disoriented birds flew into walls and fell dead on the ground. She reads it out loud, clearly thinking about the dead bird earlier in the day. She looks at me, perhaps hoping I am foolish enough to venture an opinion on the coincidence. All I know is that I can't wait to retell it.

23

My family arrives at the house, and after greet-ing me with delightful affection, my daughters' principal focus turns to their grandmother. All five grandchildren have always been very protective of her. She appears at ease, talkative, asking after their lives as usual. They take it in stride, as they are accustomed to unexpected reactions from her. They consider their grandmother an original—eccentric and grounded, for-mal and outrageous, always testing the limits of polit-ical correctness. They admire her, but she also makes them laugh, which has contributed greatly to their love for her.

The friend who flew in from Colombia asks my mom for permission to see my dad, and she agrees. I offer that choice to my daughters. One declines. The other accepts and looks at her grandfather from a distance, offering little comment, but her expression betrays curiosity com-peting with grief.

By now the news is on television, and biographies of

my father, short and long, old or hastily assembled, are running on several channels. My mother clicks back and forth between them, engrossed but without comment. We gather around her to review the life and achievements of a man who lies, deceased, a room away.

24

Two men from the mortuary are at the door. Their small van is backed into the garage and the door closed behind it. The people who work at the house mobilize quickly to say their last goodbye. The cook approaches and caresses my father's face and whispers in his ear, "*Buen viaje, Don Gabriel.*" She is not tall and strains to reach his forehead. She finally kisses his nose, then the back of his hand. My brother whispers something in my father's ear that I cannot hear. The moment is so intensely intimate it's almost unbearable. I back away and leave the room. The others stand around the bed or outside the room in silence, looking at him. My mother does not approach again.

The two men transfer my father into a body bag with surprising ease, flowers and all, then strap the bag down firmly onto a stretcher. The carrying of the stretcher out of the room and through another room and down the stairs is a breathtaking sight. In all the possible events that my imagination had offered me over the last few days, this moment was never foreseen. The men move expertly, but nothing in their demeanor betrays any excessive familiarity, let alone boredom, with a task that they have performed innumerable times, with people of all ages and in all circumstances. Their attitude imbues the task with dignity. It's what even strangers do always and everywhere for people who have died: take care of their bodies with seriousness. As he is carried down the stairs slowly, the stretcher has to be tilted until it is almost vertical, to negotiate the turn at the landing. For a moment I imagine my father upright, as if at attention, unseen and unseeing in the dark. We are all standing at the top or at the bottom of the stairs, watching in silence. Only my mother is seated, looking on, inscrutable. Unlike the death earlier, or the cremation later that evening, the feelings regarding this moment are devoid of mystery. They cut to the bone: he is leaving home, and he will never return.

As the stretcher is placed in the mortuary van, I move with my brother and our children to a window that overlooks the street. There are about two hundred people outside the house, admirers (whom my dad would rather call readers), press, and police. Neighbors watch from their windows and rooftops. The garage door opens, and the van makes its way slowly and carefully through the crowd as policemen bark orders that go mostly ignored. My daughters watch in astonishment. Their grandfather's fame is sometimes something concrete, other times abstract and far from their world in California. Once, when they were little, they walked into a restaurant in Mexico City with him, and the establishment broke out into applause. It was enchanting to hear them retell it. During my parents' stays in Los Angeles, I frequently took them out to lunch to some of the trendiest restaurants, where they ate surrounded by the local rich and famous, in anonymity. Usually it was only the Latino valet parking attendants who recognized my father, and on a couple of occasions they sent one of their own to buy books so that he could inscribe them after the meal. Nothing could give him greater pleasure.

25

When we arrive at the funeral home in the early evening, there are hundreds of people gathered out front, the crowd spilling out to the avenue. Since my father's body was delivered here, there has been the expectation that a service will be open to the public, or at least to friends. Traffic has to be diverted, and police carve out a way for our car to make it into the parking garage. Later I hear from friends that they were there.

A funeral director and the general manager of the funeral home meet us with the courteous and sober formality that is characteristic of the profession but also profoundly Mexican. We wait in an improvised seating area at one end of the underground garage, near a door that leads to the crematorium. With me are my wife, two family friends, and one of my father's aides, who was extremely attached to him (some of her coworkers speculated that she was in love with him). After several hours of conversations and news watching, innumerable phone calls and emails, and many exchanges with friends who arrived at the house in the last hours, it already feels like days have gone by since my father died. I feel numb. My mind tries several different avenues—sadness, memories, logic—they all meet shallow dead ends. A half-hearted, punchy sense of humor is the only thing I can access.

We are told it will still be a while before my father is ready for cremation. My mother's orders are clear: do it tonight, as soon as possible. So we wait.

I pick up a call from an actor friend in Los Angeles. Talking to him is a welcome break, but it also makes my life in California feel a world away. The very necessity of switching languages, which under normal circumstances I do effortlessly, feels like work this time, like playing a badly written role or trying to fool a border agent.

All of a sudden, my double life feels psychotic. No two neighboring countries, it has been said, are more different, even despite the Mexican presence in the US. It's more than language and culture; it's a state of mind and a worldview, with enviable things on both sides, but as different as the two sides of a coin. I have become as bicultural as I can imagine a person becoming, but on this day, which is so much about my father's universe, the duality feels strained.

I didn't realize until well into my forties that my decision to live and work in Los Angeles and in English was a deliberate, if unconscious, choice to make my own way beyond the sphere of influence of my father's success. It took me twenty years to see what was obvious to people around me: that I had chosen to work in a country where a language was spoken that my father couldn't speak (he was fluent in French and Italian, but only fluent enough in English to read the news), where he spent little time, had few close friends, and for years had no visa that allowed him entrance. I also chose writing and directing for film, which was his lifelong dream before failed attempts at selling his bizarre stories drove him to turn them into some of the most acclaimed novels of his century. I started off timidly, in a career as a cinematographer that was not totally unsuccessful but that eventually collapsed under the weight of other ambitions. When I was about to go into preproduction on my first film, my father asked if he could read the screenplay. I could tell that he was concerned for me, afraid as he always was that everything and anything my brother and I did would be judged against his achievements. Fortunately for both of us, he liked the screenplay. He loved my finished films and showed them off shamelessly to his friends or to anyone who could be dragged into a screening.

In his later years my father suggested we write a screenplay together, for me to direct. He had always wanted to write a film about a middle-aged woman with a successful career who suspects her husband is having an affair; she soon discovers that her husband does indeed have a lover, but it's a woman very much like herself, with similar customs and tastes, who lives in an apartment very much like theirs. In fact, he thought the same actress should play both women. But when we sat down to develop it, his diminishing memory made for frustrating conversations. They were painful for me, and so I either postponed them or cut them short, hoping he would forget. It was a while before he finally did, and he may have sometimes thought that I was simply not interested. To this day, that episode remains a source of sadness.

26

Eventually, we are asked inside the mortuary. To the right is the crematorium, and to the left is a prep room where, I am told, I can spend a few moments with my father. In that room we are met by an attractive young woman in scrubs. She shakes my hand and gives me her condolences and adds that, although it was not requested, she worked on my dad a little, and she hopes that is all right. She has applied subtle makeup on him, combed his hair, and trimmed his mustache and the unruly eyebrows that my mother brushed with her thumb innumerable times over the years. This practice of prepping the dead for viewing was disturbing to my father, like everything having to do with funereal practices. (He never attended a funeral. "I don't like to bury my friends," he'd say.) But now he looks ten years younger and merely asleep, and I am surprised by how happy I am to be able to see him like this one last time, even if it's with the help of cosmetics. The bedsheet is even more tightly wrapped around him than before, and I know in life his claustrophobia would have made it unbearable. It's the first moment that it occurs to me that he is beyond things. (He once recited poetry in his head for forty-five minutes, eyes closed, to survive the claustrophobia of a long PET scan.)

The sound of a curtain being closed makes me turn, and I realize I have been left alone in the room. I look around. Other than the gurney on which my father lies and another empty table, there is no piece of furniture or equipment in the room, which is impeccably clean and free of any odor unusual to me. I can't decide if I am in a hurry or if I am not. Both options are appealing. I touch his cheek and it's cold, but it's not an unpleasant sensation. In this calm, resting state, his features betray no signs of dementia. I am again able to read on this face his lucidity, his infinite curiosity, and the prodigious powers of concentration that I envy above all his things. He worked most days from 9 in the morning until 2:30 in the afternoon in what I can only describe as a trance. When my brother and I were children, my mother would sometimes send us into his study with a message, and he would stop writing and turn to us while we delivered it. He would look right through us, his Mediterranean eyelids at half mast, a cigarette going in one hand and another burning in the ashtray, and reply nothing. As I became older, I would sometimes add, "You have no idea what I just said, do you?" and still get no answer. Even after we walked away, he remained in that position, turned toward the door, lost in a labyrinth of narrative.

I came to believe that with that level of focus there was little one couldn't achieve. My brother, who works with acute single-mindedness on his art and design, inherited some of it.

Despite this, promptly at 2:30, our father would be sitting at lunch with us, totally present. He'd often start by announcing that he was writing the best novel since the great Russian novels of the nineteenth century, then move on to any and all subjects, often interrogating us about our day. After the afternoon nap his enthusiasm began to weaken. By dinner time he would comment that the next day's work was difficult, that it included a couple of serious hurdles, and that clearing them was crucial to the creative success of the book. By breakfast the next morning he was frank about his new level of worry: "If today doesn't go well, the whole novel might be a bust. If that's the case, I would abandon it." Later, at lunch, the cycle would begin again.

It dawns on me suddenly that he's not breathing, and it's spellbinding. Then I'm afraid that he might breathe and that a dead man breathing would be monstrous, and so I watch him closely for a few long seconds until I realize that I am holding my own breath, so I exhale quickly and feel ridiculous. His mustache is as his as the nose and the eyes and the lips. It's his first and only mustache, the one he grew out at age seventeen and never shaved. He lost it during chemotherapy in his early seventies, but it grew back, like a lizard's tail. I'm trying to build bridges in my mind between my living father and my dead father and my famous father and this father here in front of me, and I'm failing. I have an instinct to say something, and I think of it: "Well done." But I don't say it out loud for fear of sounding earnest or sentimental. I want to take a photograph of him and I do so with my phone. Instantly I feel sick to my stomach with guilt and shame for having violated his privacy so violently. I delete the photograph and instead take one of the roses on his body. He would have been delighted that the pretty young woman worked on him. He would have flirted with her.

27

I draw back the curtain and say that we should go on. He is pushed by an attendant from one room to the next, a distance of less than twenty steps. I am momentarily reminded of the short distance traveled by men condemned to death who are sitting in a holding cell and, when the time comes, realize that the execution chamber has been there all along, behind the wall. The room is larger than the previous one but also scrupulously clean. My father's aide and the two friends are there, but my wife has returned outside to the sitting area. I rush out and wave her back in impatiently, and I don't know if it's because I need support or because I refuse to accept her self-effacing ways. Who the hell knows? I want her in there with me and that's that, and it's mighty male of me to never consider that she may not want to witness the cremation of her father-in-law.

The attendant lines up the gurney with the closed doors of the chamber, and for a moment nothing happens. Only the low, discreet hum of the burners can be heard from inside the impeccable, polite machine, awaiting their turn to do the voracious work. Then someone either gives me a look or says something to me (I can no longer remember) that implies that there is no proceeding until I say so. I signal to the funeral director that we are ready, and an operator opens the doors of the chamber and my father is slowly transported inside by a short conveyor belt. My father's aide says, *"Adiós, jefe."* The funeral home workers clap. The yellow roses are still on him, and I remember thinking they would be annihilated in an instant. The body travels until only the head and shoulders remain visible, and then something goes awry and it becomes stuck. One of the funeral home employees walks up quickly and efficiently, as if this occurrence were not unusual, and pushes on both shoulders firmly until the body moves again and is finally engulfed. The doors shut behind it.

The sight of my father's body entering the cremation chamber is mesmerizing and numbing. It feels both impossibly pregnant and meaningless. The only thing I can feel with any certainty at that moment is that he is not there at all. It remains the most impenetrable image of my life.

PART FOUR

. . . volando entre el rumor oscuro de las últimas hojas heladas de su otoño hacia la patria de tinieblas de la verdad del olvido, agarrado de miedo a los trapos de hilachas podridas del balandrán de la muerte y ajeno a los clamores de las muchedumbres frenéticas que se echaban a las calles cantando . . .

                                        —El otoño del patriarca

. . . flying through the dark sound of the last frozen leaves of his autumn toward the homeland of shadows of the truth of oblivion, clinging to his fear of the rotting cloth of death's hooded cassock and alien to the clamor of the frantic crowds who took to the streets singing . . .

—*The Autumn of the Patriarch*

28

The following day, Friday, a morning earthquake reminds us that the world goes on. For our visitors from places free of earthquakes, it only adds to the hallucinatory nature of their trip. A little later, my mother receives a call notifying her that Bellas Artes—the National Institute of Fine Arts—would like to hold a memorial for my father, open to the public, with the presidents of Mexico and Colombia in attendance. We are happy to do it, but it can't be denied that waiting almost four more days before starting to turn the page will be difficult.

Friends continue to arrive from near and far. The house turns into a cocktail party, a wake with drinks and snacks around the clock and my mother holding court, cajoling, interrogating, passing judgment, indefatigable. There are even people I've heard about but never met, friends my parents have made over the last few years, after I moved to Los Angeles. The group reflects their interests: all ages, occupations, and social strata. My mother meets with the occasional guest separately and in private, among them two ex-presidents. Despite her grief, and one must assume her exhaustion, she is cordial and patient. One or two of the visitors she judges harshly after they leave, with a little bitterness and cutting humor. She is not forgiving of anyone who stopped calling after my father lost his faculties, even if just to say hello to her. That shit list is short, but if you're on it, good luck.

On another occasion, my brother is told that the president of a major university is at the door. When the door is opened, the man steps forward, delivers a well-constructed if stodgy eulogy, reminiscent of a political stump speech, embraces my brother formally without another word, and departs forever.

One of my father's brothers and his wife arrive, as well as a cousin from that side of the family whom I haven't seen in almost twenty years. Raised in Cartagena, she now lives in a small town in Maine, married to a local, and her stories of adapting the local culture to her, rather than the other way around, are great fun. They are a reminder of my father's family's passion for anecdote, embellishment, and exaggeration. Grab your listeners and never let them go. A good story trumps the truth, always. A good story is the truth.

One afternoon his secretary calls me. She's worried that everyone at the hospital supply rental company knows my dad passed away in that bed. It could end up anywhere, she adds, sold off or collected as a morbid memento. We decide to buy the bed. For the time being it's disassembled and placed, until we decide what to do with it, in the garage at the back of the house, out of sight. We say nothing to my mother, who wouldn't want it around. She'd say it's there waiting for her to be next.

My brother retrieves from the funeral home an urn with our father's ashes. Picking the right urn had been a predicament. My mother wanted something neither expensive nor cheap, elegant but discreet. It appears to pass muster when she sees it, though she does only for a second or two. Her instructions are to put it away in my father's study until the memorial, and she provides a yellow silk scarf to wrap it in. Then, in what can only be attributed to my own exhaustion, it occurs to me that it's a good idea for my daughters and my brother's children to pose with the urn. They are appalled but also find the proposition hysterical, so they do it, mortified and fighting off laughter. What can you do but laugh at the thought of your grandfather reduced to three pounds of ash?

The party lasts the full three days, and it's lifesaving, if tiring. On Monday, the day of the memorial, I sit alone at the breakfast table. I look up from my plate to discover a perfect little rainbow forming on the backrest of my father's chair. The morning sunlight, refracted by the same glass wall that killed the bird a few days earlier, is the source. By midafternoon Monday, the core of the group, a few dozen people, congregate in the garden for a photograph before boarding a fleet of cars and taxis for Bellas Artes. As the group disbands in the garden, my mother calls out her marching orders: "*¡Aquí nadie llora!*" Nobody's allowed to cry.

On the drive to Bellas Artes, I ask a friend if he can carry the urn as we make our way out of the vehicles and into the palace. I don't want to be photographed carrying it, for no other reason than the action is too private for me to want to see it in the news.

We gather where the cars drop us off, and we follow the director of the institute upstairs and through halls until we reach a door and step out, quite unexpectedly, into the main hall. I don't know what I anticipated, but what awaits is intimidating. On one level is a large base where the urn is placed, surrounded by yellow roses. To either side are two large areas of rows of chairs for guests. But facing the urn is a scaffolding with over a hundred photographers, videographers, and reporters. We sit in the first row of the area to our left, among dignitaries and friends who arrived earlier. It's clear that we are expected to stand guard around the urn, for a few minutes. My brother and I walk with my mother and stand where we are told. The barrage of camera flashes makes a very odd moment surreal. It's impossible not to think of people we know who might be watching from around the world. It's not really me who's there, just this guy in a suit and tie, somewhere between the ages of three and fifty-three, trying his best not to draw attention to himself. After us, my brother's family stands guard, and eventually my wife and daughters. One of the girls, who suffers from social anxiety, tells me later that she found the experience very painful, almost unbearably so. I feel for her. To be exposed like that, in a most private moment, in sad circumstances, and in the throes of adolescence, must be torture.

For the next two hours we sit and watch while thousands of people, most of whom have been standing for hours outside in the drizzle, walk through, paying their respects. Many place flowers, mementos, religious figures, or pendants at the base of the platform where the urn sits. Many also drop off my father's books, or notes of condolence or love, some addressed to maestro, but most, more informally, to Gabo or Gabito. It's a firm reminder that he also very much belonged to other people.

The event offers a chance to see a whole new group of friends we hadn't seen yet, or for a long time. I even spot a few passing by who walk in with the mourners. I signal to them to meet me on the other side of the main hall, and we catch up quickly. Thanks to these encounters, it turns out to be a not unenjoyable event.

At one point, sitting with my own thoughts, I look more carefully at the faces of mourners passing by. I find myself remembering that my father used to say that everyone has three lives: the public, the private, and the secret. For a moment it occurs to me that perhaps someone from his secret life could be among these people. Before I can dwell on that too much, a *trío vallenato* that has stood in line arrives, stops, and plays a song to my father. It's festive and welcome.

We hear that the Colombian president's airplane has landed and that he is already on his way to the event. He soon makes his entrance behind his host, the president of Mexico. A pleasant surprise is that many friends of my parents came on that plane, and this new wave lifts our spirits again. My mother greets them with great glee, unabashedly delighted. "*¿Qué te parece todo esto?*" she asks. (How about this?)

The national anthems of both countries are played, which changes the mood. The Colombian president, who is close to me in age, is someone my dad knew for years, and they were friends long before he became president. He doesn't mince words. Gabo, he says, is simply the greatest Colombian who ever lived. My mom watches him with pride, like he's a nephew who has done well. His brother is also there, a journalist who is one of my mother's favorite people and who catches her up on the gossip in Bogotá. She's happy, all things considered.

Toward the end of the Mexican president's address, which is otherwise quite good, he refers to us as "the sons and the widow." I squirm in my seat, sure that my mother will disapprove. When the heads of state leave, my brother walks over to me and deadpans, "The widow." We laugh nervously. Later my mom speaks her opinion in no uncertain terms, grumpily. She threatens to tell the

first journalist who crosses her path that she plans to re-
marry as soon as possible. Her last words on the subject
are "*No soy la viuda. Yo soy yo.*" (I am not the widow.
I am me.)

My brother and I had promised ourselves that as long
as people were standing in line outside Bellas Artes to
pay their respects to our father, he and I would stay no
matter how late, beyond the departure of heads of state,
press, friends, and family. But moments after the event is
officially over, it's clear to us that our good intentions are
not enough to keep us from the verge of collapse. So, disappointed by our failure but hoping to forgive ourselves,
we leave.

29

I fly back to Los Angeles for a couple of days. Until very recently, even when he was unaware of who I was, my father would be disappointed whenever I said goodbye. *"No, hombre, ¿por qué te vas? Quédate. No me dejes."* (No, man, why are you leaving? Stay. Don't leave me.) It was always a kick in the ass—not unlike dropping off a crying child at preschool, but without the conviction, misguided or not, that it's all for their own good.

At home there are already hundreds of letters of condolences waiting. In this other reality they seem to refer to an event that happened far away and long ago. I leave them for later, when I might (and eventually do) find them nourishing. On a call with my mother, she tells me that a man came to the door, announcing himself as Mr. Porrúa. She assumes he is someone from the same Porrúa family that owns one of the oldest publishing houses in Mexico. She receives him in the living room and doesn't recognize him, but he is friendly and effusive, asks after my father's secretary, my brother, and me all by name, and shares his memories of my father. When the secretary walks in, he jumps to his feet and embraces her effusively. She is too embarrassed to admit she doesn't remember him. Mr. Porrúa sits again and soon explains that he drove into town in a car that has now broken down. Determined to convey his feelings, he got a lift from a friend who is waiting outside. Would my mother be kind enough to lend him the equivalent of about two hundred US dollars to get his car fixed? My mother gives him cash, the man leaves, and he is never heard from again. Later we discover he is a known con man. She has a good laugh about it.

Apart from condolences, mail arrives from friends sending me the front pages of newspapers the world over from the day of my father's death. That takes me into the rabbit hole of the internet, where I see that virtually every front page of any national or regional paper carried the news that day. I read as many versions as I can, each paper stressing different aspects of his life or achievements. Once again, I struggle to reconcile this person in print with the one I've spent the last few weeks with—ailing, dying, ashes in a box—and with my childhood dad, the one who eventually became my child and my brother's. I read through my notes of the last few days, torn about whether to bring them together in some kind of narrative. Like my mother, my dad held fast to their belief that our home life was strictly private. As kids we were held to that standard over and over again. But we are not kids anymore. Old children, perhaps, but not kids.

My father complained that one of the things he hated most about death was that it would be the only aspect of his life he would not be able to write about. Everything he lived through, witnessed, and thought was in his books, fictionalized or ciphered. "If you can live without writing, don't write," he often said. I am among those who cannot live without writing, so I trust he would be forgiving. Another of his pronouncements that I will take to my own grave is this: "There is nothing better than something well written." That one is particularly resonant, as I am aware that whatever I write concerning his last days can easily find publication, regardless of its quality. Deep down I know I will write and show these recollections in some form or another. If I have to, I will seek refuge in yet another thing he said to us: "When I'm dead, do whatever you want."

30

I return to Mexico to spend time with my mother and to see friends from Barcelona who were not able to fly earlier. We have been close to them since 1968, and now that the cocktail party is over, it's mostly just us in the house. It's good to enjoy them in relative peace and quiet, but it also makes my father's absence more evident. They are both therapists, and they were two of my father's main confidants. He was never in therapy, arguing that the typewriter was his analyst. Whether he was afraid that therapy would take away even a sliver of his creativity or was uneasy with the undressing that may come with it, we'll never know. He did sometimes encourage us to talk to close friends or family about our worries, or we would end up paying a professional to listen to them.

My main desire during this visit is to talk to my father about his own death and its aftermath. I stop by his study in the back of the garden, where his ashes are locked away in a cabinet and where, as with the rest of the house, a return to normality is creeping back in, slowly but relentlessly. My mother hasn't returned to the study, and never will. The room where my father died has returned to its old form. Among my daughters, niece, and nephews, it's a room to be avoided. I decide to sleep there in an attempt to renormalize it as a guest room. I spend an uneventful night, for better or worse.

31

I board an early flight back to Los Angeles. It's my eighth
flight to or from Mexico City in three weeks. As the
aircraft taxies slowly toward the runway, I am suddenly
overwhelmed by the clarity with which I can feel that
my father's magnificent time on earth has passed. During
takeoff I am filled with sorrow, but the unexpected cou-
pling of the emptiness of loss with the powerful energy
of the engines is strangely exhilarating. As the landing
gear retracts and the airplane banks left, two volcanoes
can be seen to the east, backlit by the rising sun: Popo-
catepetl, hundreds of thousands of years older than the
written word, and Ixtacihuatl, lying in state. As we reach
ten thousand feet, a bell chimes like a gentle alarm clock.
I recline my seat and look around. The woman next to me
is reading *One Hundred Years of Solitude* on her phone.

PART FIVE

El capitán miró a Fermina Daza y vio en sus pestañas los primeros destellos de una escarcha invernal. Luego miró a Florentino Ariza, su dominio invencible, su amor impávido, y lo asustó la sospecha tardía de que es la vida, más que la muerte, la que no tiene límites.

—*El amor en los tiempos del cólera*

The captain looked at Fermina Daza and saw on her eyelashes the first glimmer of wintry frost. Then he looked at Florentino Ariza, his invincible power, his intrepid love, and he was overwhelmed by the belated suspicion that it is life, more than death, that has no limits.

—Love in the Time of Cholera

32

Our mother died in August 2020. It all happened more or less as we thought it might, given that, after sixty-five years of smoking, her lung capacity was ever diminishing and in her last years she was on oxygen around the clock. Her spirits, however, never waned. She watched news on television for several hours a day while checking other news on a tablet and staying in touch with her global web of friends through two landlines and three cell phones lined up in front of her. In her last few months we chatted on video almost every day, and although there was little to report beyond world events, she seemed like her old self, if a little bored to be isolated from most of her cronies. Even in declining health and with diminishing mobility, she did not seem overly anxious about her condition. I couldn't see major cracks in her demeanor. Was it fearlessness, denial, or pretense? She excelled in all three areas at different times.

"When do you think this pandemic will be over?" she asked me often. It's late 2020 now, and I still wouldn't have an answer for her. Unable to travel, I saw her alive for the last time on the cracked screen of my phone, and again five minutes later, gone forever. Two brief live videos, separated by eternity, from which my capacity for storytelling has yet to recuperate. What can I possibly recount that has any more power? In the days following her death I expected her to call me to ask, "So what was it like, my death? No, slow down. Sit. Tell it properly." She'd listen, I imagine, alternating laughter with greedy hits of the cigarettes that killed her. She'd talk to friends the world over, receive their condolences with amusement and bright vanity, before inquiring, with greater interest, about a child's divorce or an object stolen.

My father had pressured her for years to quit smoking, and she tried a few times, very reluctantly, but failed. Even in her early days on oxygen she sometimes asked me to hold the mask in my hand while she took a few puffs of a cigarette. "Don't turn the machine off," she would say. "I'll be right back on it." My father's warnings of what the death of a smoker could be haunted my brother and me forever. Those worries proved useful, however, because we (or I should say my brother, who was on the ground with her) were very vigilant that her exit not be painful or racked with anxiety. It was neither.

Most of my father's drafts of work in progress were salvaged by my mother behind his back, because he was firmly against showing or preserving unfinished work. Many times during our childhood, my brother and I were summoned to sit on the floor of his study and help him rip up entire previous versions and throw them out—an unhappy image, I am sure, for collectors and students of his process. His papers and his reference library went to the Harry Ransom Center in Austin, Texas, and my mom took great pleasure in the opening ceremonies of that collection. Both my brother's family and mine were there, and she enjoyed and took shelter in the company of her grandchildren. The granddaughters gave her particular pleasure, I suppose, because as the grandkids grew older the girls remained more interested in her daily concerns and followed her health issues more closely. She gifted them with her old handbags and accessories, sometimes so generously that the girls were uneasy to accept them. But not too uneasy. One of my daughters felt that my mother was the person in the world that she most resembled and found that a source of pride, and my niece was, among us all, arguably the most physically present in her last years. My other daughter was very diligent in reaching out to her from abroad with regularity and was very affectionate with her. My mother's own grandmother had been a towering figure in her life, a matriarch respected and feared, and that, I believe, contributed to her weakness for granddaughters. She loved my brother's sons, but she believed that boys tended to retreat into their own worlds as they grew older, and she accepted it. These are only my theories, of course, and if she heard them she would scoff at them, turning away from me impatiently.

Two years after my father's death, we took his ashes to Cartagena. They were placed inside the base of a bust (uncanny in its resemblance to him), in the courtyard of a colonial building, now open to the public. There was an official ceremony, preceded and followed by the obligatory open-house cocktail party at my parents' house. Like the one around the time of my father's death, it went on for several days, but since the mood was more jovial, my mother made sure there was live music late into the night. I found the days somewhat emotional and perhaps a little tiring but, curiously, I thought at the time, not too much. It all seemed quite bearable. On my final day there, I stopped early in the morning at the courtyard for one last look at the resting place of the ashes. It was stunning to think they would be there, that he would be there, for a very long time, centuries perhaps, long after everyone now living was gone. The ride to the airport was a sad one, and twenty-four hours after landing in Bogotá I was hospitalized with a bladder infection and a blood clot in my leg. Perhaps the previous days had been more stressful than I thought.

It's been only three months since my mother died, and I am surprised by how quickly her stature has grown for me. I am unable to walk past a photograph of her without spending a moment looking at it. Her face seems kinder and more beautiful than ever, even in old age. A lifelong sufferer of anxiety (and perhaps unaware of it), she was nevertheless enormously capable of enjoyment.

Her interest (like my father's) in life itself and in the lives of others was inexhaustible. My feelings about my father, though loving, were complicated by his fame and talent, which made him several people that I've had to work to integrate into one, always bouncing back and forth between mixed emotions. There are also complicated feelings regarding the long, painful goodbye that was his loss of memory, and the guilt of finding some satisfaction in feeling temporarily more mentally powerful than him. My feelings toward my mother are now, surprisingly, utterly uncomplicated. This is the kind of statement that makes therapists raise their eyebrows, and yet it's true. She was afraid of big expressions of emotion, and in our childhood she encouraged us to keep a stiff upper lip. But with time I came to understand that this was a condition that she inherited from her parents, who very likely inherited it themselves. She didn't even know she was afflicted with it, and whenever I suggested she might benefit from therapy or medication, her reaction was unequivocal: "*No. No soy una histérica.*" (No. I am not a hysteric.)

I am thankful that I was able to understand this while she was still alive, and to accept it, and so what is left is only affection and an infatuation with the life force that emanated from her. She was frank and secretive, critical and indulgent, brave, but afraid of disorder. She could be prickly and judgmental but also quick to forgive, especially when a person shared their troubles with her. Then she was on their side forever and won over their devotion.

With my brother and me, she was not physical, but profoundly affectionate in her attitude, increasingly so as the years went by. Her complex personality has surely contributed to my lifelong fascination with women, especially multifaceted women, enigmatic women, and what are often referred to, I think unfairly, as difficult women.

I have a renewed admiration for my parents. I admit that this perspective (some would call it revisionism) is not uncommon. Absence makes us grow fonder and more forgiving, and we recognize that our parents were walking on feet of clay like everybody else. In my mother's case, I am amazed at how, given the period and place she was born into, she grew into the person she became, holding her own or even commanding the world that my father's success offered them. She was a woman of her time, with no higher education, a mother, a wife and homemaker, but many younger women with big lives and successful careers openly admired and envied her grit, her resilience, and her sense of herself. She was known by her friends as *La Gaba*, a nickname based on my father's Gabo and therefore patriarchal, and yet no one who knew her believed she had grown into anything but a great version of herself.

In a restaurant two years before her death, my mom told me that after her, the first born, her mother had two babies who died in infancy. I was surprised that I had never heard this. I asked if she had any recollection of it, and she said yes. She remembered clearly her mother holding a dead baby in her arms. She cradled her left arm, showing me how.

"Why haven't you told me this before?" I inquired.

"Because you never asked," she replied. Silly me. Sometime later I asked about it again, hungry for more details, but she denied not only having told such a story but also that she had ever seen a deceased baby sibling. I was dumbstruck. This was not senility or dementia. Her memory was always ironclad. I insisted. "No. It never happened," she said with finality. I let it go that day, but I was resolved to return to that mystery again in the future, in case the wind had changed, but time ran out.

I also spent fifty years of my life not knowing that my father had no vision in the center of his left eye. I found out while accompanying him to the ophthalmologist, and only because the doctor mentioned it after the exam.

I wish I knew how my parents remembered their younger selves, or that I had even an inkling of what they thought of their place in the world, back when their lives were confined by the small towns of their Colombian childhoods. I would give anything to spend an hour with my father when he was a rascal of nine, or with my mother when she was a spirited girl of eleven, both unable to suspect the extraordinary lives that awaited them. And so, in the back of my mind is the preoccupation that perhaps I didn't know them well enough, and I certainly regret that I didn't ask them more about the fine print of their lives, their most private thoughts, their greatest hopes and fears. It's possible that they felt the same about us, for who can fully know their own children? I am eager for my brother's thoughts on this, since I am sure a home is a very different place for each one of its inhabitants.

A decision regarding the future of the house awaits us. My brother and I are enthusiastic about visiting the house museums of writers and artists of the past, and of other unhappy successful people of that ilk, so we are leaning in that direction. I am a little surprised, nevertheless, by my willingness to open the doors of our own family home to anyone and everyone. Perhaps it's a desperate stab at defeating the passage of time, or at least at sparing us the heartache of having to empty it and sell it to strangers.

The death of the second parent is like looking through a telescope one night and no longer finding a planet that has always been there. It has vanished, with its religion, its customs, its own peculiar habits and rituals, big and small. The echo remains. I think of my father every morning when I dry my back with a towel the way he taught me after seeing me struggling with it at the age of six. Much of his advice is always with me. (A favorite: be forgiving of your friends, so that they may be forgiving of you.) I remember my mother each time I walk a guest to the front door when they're leaving, because not to do so would be inexcusable, and whenever I pour olive oil on anything. And in recent years, the three of us look back at me from my face in the mirror. I've also endeavored to guide my life by their seldom spoken but unimpeachable rule: do not be crooked.

Much of our parents' culture survives in some form in the new planets created by my brother and me with our families. Some of it has merged with what our wives brought, or chose not to bring, from their own tribes. With the years, the splintering will continue, and life will lay upon my parents' world layers and layers of other lives lived, until the day comes when nobody on this earth holds the memory of their physical presence. I am now almost the age my father was when I asked him what he thought about at night, after turning out the lights. Like him, I am not too worried yet, but I am more aware of time than ever. For now, I am still here, thinking of them.

ACKNOWLEDGMENTS

I would like to thank:

My wife, Adriana, and my daughters, Isabel and Ines.

My sister-in-law, Pía, and my niece and nephews Emilia, Mateo, and Jerónimo.

The many friends, employees of my parents, doctors, and nurses that I referred to in the book.

Luis Miguel Palomares, Luis and Leticia Feduchi, Mónica Alonso, Cristóbal Pera, Sofía Ortiz, Diego García Elio, Maribel Luque, Javier Martín, Neena Beber, Amy Lippman, Julie Lynn, Bonnie Curtis, Paul Attanasio, Nick Kazan, Robin Swicord, Sarah Treem, Jorge F. Hernández, and Jon and Barbara Avnet.

PHOTOGRAPHS

Gabo at 13 or 14.
He was already a *chévere*. A dandy.

Mercedes at 17.
That face says it all.

In the late 1960s, when
smoking was still good for you.

Gonzalo, Gabo, Rodrigo.
Los Angeles, 2008.

October 12th, 1982,
the morning the Nobel prize was announced.

October 12th, 2012,
thirty years later, same place, same tree,
same robe for the occasion.

Who would dare say
old people aren't beautiful?

Calle Fuego 144.
The worst-kept secret in town.

Gabo at home, taking his Tuesday nap
under a large Colombian ruana.

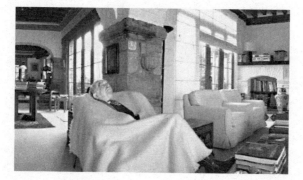

Gabo's study since 1976.

Mercedes's 80th birthday celebration.

With my brother, Gonzalo, our families,
and Mercedes, aka *El Cocodrilo Sagrado*
(The Sacred Crocodile), *La Madre Santa* (The Holy
Mother), *La Jefa Máxima* (The Boss Supreme).

Gabo leaves home.

Mercedes and Gabo's *ofrenda*,
November 2020, Year of the Plague.

CHRONOLOGY

1927   Gabriel García Márquez is born on March 6, 1927,
to Gabriel Eligio García and Luisa Santiaga Márquez
in Aracataca, Colombia. The eldest child of a large
family, he spends his early years living with his maternal
grandparents. His grandfather, a former colonel, would
later inspire García Márquez's novella *No One Writes to
the Colonel*.

1936   After his grandfather's death, García Márquez goes to
live with his parents in Sucre.

1940   García Márquez moves with his family to the port city
of Barranquilla and starts high school.

1947   García Márquez studies law at the National University
in Bogotá. Two of his short stories are published in the
newspaper *El Espectador*.

1948–50   After two years of political conflict in Colombia,
riots force the National University to close. García
Márquez returns to Barranquilla, where he works as a
journalist. He starts writing his first novel, *Leaf Storm*.

1954   García Márquez is hired to write for *El Espectador*.
He publishes a series of articles about a Colombian
sailor who survived a high-seas shipwreck, which causes
controversy in Colombia.

1955–57   *Leaf Storm* is published in 1955. García Márquez
moves to Paris to work as a foreign correspondent. During
this period, he travels to the Eastern bloc countries to
report on various issues.

1958   García Márquez returns to Colombia. He marries
Mercedes Barcha in Barranquilla. They remain married
until his death.

1959   García Márquez travels to Cuba as a rank and
file journalist to cover the Cuban Revolution for a
Colombian newspaper. Mercedes gives birth to their first
son, Rodrigo.

1960–61   García Márquez lives in NY briefly as
correspondent of the Cuban press agency Prensa Latina
before moving his family to Mexico. His novel *No One
Writes to the Colonel* is published in 1961.

1962–66   The couple's second son, Gonzalo, is born in 1962.
García Márquez spends eighteen months writing *One
Hundred Years of Solitude*.

1967   *One Hundred Years of Solitude* is published in June.
The book is an immediate success, selling millions of
copies worldwide and earning García Márquez much
acclaim. The family moves to Spain.

1975   *The Autumn of the Patriarch* is published.

1979–81   García Márquez divides his time between Colombia and Mexico. He begins writing *Chronicle of a Death Foretold*.

1982   García Márquez wins the Noble Prize for Literature.

1983–87   *Love in the Time of Cholera* is published in 1985. García Márquez helps establish the International Film School in Cuba. *Chronicle of a Death Foretold* is adapted for film, directed by Francesco Rosi.

1989   *The General in His Labyrinth* is published.

1994   García Márquez helps establish the Foundation for New Ibero-American Journalism to support democratic, independent journalism in Latin America.

1996   *News of a Kidnapping*, a nonfiction account of several kidnapping cases in Colombia by drug lord Pablo Escobar, is published.

1999   García Márquez battles lymphatic cancer. He goes into remission.

2002–04   His memoir, *Living to Tell the Tale*, is published in 2002. His final novel, *Memories of My Melancholy Whores*, is published two years later.

2010–12   Rumors circulate that García Márquez is writing a new novel, but his younger brother, Jaime, denies the reports. It is revealed to the public that the author is suffering from dementia and can no longer write.

2014   García Márquez dies at his home in Mexico City.

2020   Mercedes Barcha dies in Mexico City.

SELECTED BIBLIOGRAPHY

No One Writes to the Colonel, and Other Stories. Translated from the Spanish by J. S. Bernstein. New York: Harper & Row, 1968.

One Hundred Years of Solitude. Translated from the Spanish by Gregory Rabassa. New York: Harper & Row, 1970.

Leaf Storm, and Other Stories. Translated from the Spanish by Gregory Rabassa. New York: Harper & Row, 1972.

The Autumn of the Patriarch. Translated from the Spanish by Gregory Rabassa. New York: Harper & Row, 1976.

Innocent Eréndira, and Other Stories. Translated from the Spanish by Gregory Rabassa. New York: Harper & Row, 1978.

In Evil Hour. Translated from the Spanish by Gregory Rabassa. New York: Harper & Row, 1979.

Chronicle of a Death Foretold. Translated from the Spanish by Gregory Rabassa. New York: Knopf, 1983.

Collected Stories. Translated from the Spanish by J. S. Bernstein and Gregory Rabassa. New York: Harper & Row, 1984.

The Story of a Shipwrecked Sailor. Translated from the Spanish by Randolph Hogan. New York: Knopf, 1986.

Clandestine in Chile: The Adventures of Miguel Littín. Translated from the Spanish by Asa Zatz. New York: Holt, 1987.

Love in the Time of Cholera. Translated from the Spanish by Edith Grossman. New York: Knopf, 1988.

The General in His Labyrinth. Translated from the Spanish by Edith Grossman. New York: Knopf, 1990.

Collected Novellas. Translated from the Spanish by J. S. Bernstein and Gregory Rabassa. New York: HarperCollins, 1990.

Strange Pilgrims: Twelve Stories. Translated from the Spanish by Edith Grossman. New York: Knopf, 1993.

Of Love and Other Demons. Translated from the Spanish by Edith Grossman. New York: Knopf, 1995.

News of a Kidnapping. Translated from the Spanish by Edith Grossman. New York: Knopf, 1997.

Living to Tell the Tale. Translated from the Spanish by Edith Grossman. New York: Knopf, 2003.

Memories of My Melancholy Whores. Translated from the Spanish by Edith Grossman. New York: Knopf, 2005.

The Scandal of the Century, and Other Writings. Translated from the Spanish by Anne McLean. New York: Knopf, 2019.

ABOUT THE AUTHOR

Rodrigo Garcia was born in Colombia, grew up in Mexico City, and attended Harvard University. His feature films as a writer and director include *Nine Lives*, *Albert Nobbs*, and *Four Good Days*. Garcia has directed television series such as *Six Feet Under*, *The Sopranos*, and the pilot of *Big Love*, for which he received an Emmy nomination. He also directed several episodes for HBO's *In Treatment*, where, in addition to director, he served as a writer, executive producer, and series showrunner. Garcia currently resides in Los Angeles with his family.

A NOTE ON THE COVER

In creating this cover, I wanted to show the tenderness of memory and the depth of loss. I chose collage for its ephemeral qualities. Working with cut paper is a delicate process, and, as in life, things don't always go as planned. Paper is sensitive material; it can be ripped, destroyed, degraded with only a touch. The empty silhouettes of Gabriel and Mercedes, cut from an old photo, demonstrate how collage is powered by absence. Even though the form itself is about assembly and reconstruction, the gaps and voids inevitably left during the process give collage greater meaning. Combined with a reinterpretation of the couples' garden and blooming yellow roses (García Márquez's favorite flower), I sought to capture the book's reflective mood and elegiac tone.

—Alicia Tatone

Here ends Rodrigo Garcia's
A Farewell to Gabo and Mercedes.

The first edition of this book was printed
and bound at LSC Communications in
Harrisonburg, Virginia, June 2021.

A NOTE ON THE TYPE

The text of this novel was set in Sabon, an old-style serif
typeface created by Jan Tschichold between 1964 and
1967. He drew inspiration for it from the elegant and
highly legible designs of the famed sixteenth-century Pa-
risian typographer and publisher Claude Garamond and
named it after Jacques Sabon, one of Garamond's close
collaborators. Sabon has remained a popular typeface in
book design for its quintessential smooth and clean look.

HarperVia

An imprint dedicated to publishing international voices,
offering readers a chance to encounter other lives and other
points of view via the language of the imagination.